No Beautiful

Books by Anne Marie Rooney

Spitshine
No Beautiful

No Beautiful

Anne Marie Rooney

Carnegie Mellon University Press
Pittsburgh 2018

Acknowledgments

Thank you to the editors of the following journals, in which many of these poems first appeared: *Adrienne, American Poetry Review, The Awl, Better, Black Warrior Review, Colorado Review, Crazyhorse, Devil's Lake, DIAGRAM, Finery, The Journal, jubilat, La Vague, Meridian, Phoebe, Poor Claudia, Quarterly West, Salt Hill, So to Speak, The Spectacle, West Branch*, and *Witness*. Thank you, too, to Flying Object and Devil's Lake, which published poems as broadsides.

Thank you to the Barbara Deming Memorial Fund for providing a generous grant during the early stages of this book.

Most of all, thank you, immeasurably, to the communities who sustained me and sustain me, especially: Melissa Dickey, Megan McHugh, Jenn Marie Nunes, Kristin Sanders, Jerika Marchan, Carrie Chappell, Abi Pollokoff, Aran Donovan. Lillian-Yvonne Bertram, Ben Pelhan, Atom Atkinson, S.E. Smith, Zachary Harris. Rosana Cruz, Caitlin Shroyer-Ladeira, Holly Woodie, Maria Landrum. Claire Mehling, Paige Valente. Kate Ryan, Danielle Katvan, Serena Matt. Serena Chaudhry, Bess Hart, Laura Scholz, Cara Heart. Jerry Costanzo, Cynthia Lamb, Connie Amoroso, Lo Kwa Mei-en, Cecilia Vicuña, Claudia Rankine, Kiki Smith.

And forever to my family, most especially to Julia, and always Tom.

Kiki Smith
Rising, 2010
ink, mica and glitter on Nepalese paper
33" x 20-1/4" (83.8 cm x 51.4 cm)
Photograph by Kerry Ryan McFate, courtesy Pace Gallery
© Kiki Smith, courtesy Pace Gallery

Book design by Juliana Schnerr

Library of Congress Control Number 2018935068
ISBN 978-0-88748-640-1

10 9 8 7 6 5 4 3 2 1

Contents

I made a book like a rock you could slide down.
To oil an animal closer to death.
Further.
In earth, which is black mud.
Of course I move darkly.
Creep book, infinity book.
Word at the river of night.
And black mud book.
Stars or bells on water moved across.
Slick of spilled night.
Where is the separateness.
My book was riding
Across.
So what is the center.
The staple. Heat of moment
On noon and thus.
A little groveling, mouth noise.
I step closer to the frayed back needle.
Become so vast, so vast.
Then I stopped writing the poem with my breath.

Palinode

I'm sorry I was such a freaky witch.
And cut my face. I'm sorry belly shirts
to the dissection.
Little legs uncrossed at spiders,
the *Are we getting our mothers*
stuck on? to sorry.
A certain red shirt. I was roots
of moss blond.
Sorry pink and black capped
the party, sorry learning by choking
to swallow. *Stomp stomp*
I went in boots. Dude said he'd loot
my sorry neck.
Through the window
I was bent but just. Light on camel
light; apartments of lip and snarly.
I'm sorry my safety pin slip.
Sorry, stairwell.
I put my cut over the cheapo
flick fire.
Even peed in classrooms.
Sorries were flowers how I rose them:
It was ~~the cat did this~~   ~~my hatred~~
~~love~~ blood.
Sorry, cat.
I circled the fat in flame
sharpie, drew the sun about the thick,
even steed.
O sound: A net
my leg rubbed soft was sorry,
I'm running that sorry to the wound

Overture

The spirited chip and whorl. The centenary. The girls barking
in rooms. No one on a corner who sings. And air-drying
and entered. I have not been unhated. When I read the words, I sunk
listing higher. Mountains that moved, the building. Soundwork flinched
into its sentence, again. What's gained. The embodied. A sparkle on rawly
wedding. Snow which has climbed, been climbed. The intranasal spackle.
Of playoffs. Pet peeves. Bubble twins enstirring woods, a witch. Has writhing
clammed the big one, which. Not hated. And pleased. A little seldom silvered
on the burrowed down then lifted. Hurried to sense. Sensate. I was separate
from the anchor here, was cinched to the waste

My year with flowers, unshrinking

(nor were they much for winking. In that way, we were similar,
the meat and I, our faces full of twitches, rhyme-hinged on awkward
hitches. Our expenses were expansive, like, excuse me, we'd better
have it: gold wallops, white eggs, even the sterling shone
over-basket. Got water? It showed, that slouch. Little tick marks
smeared the day with been-blown kisses. Sure, we were angry,
and lonely, overmouthed. Our stains showed only in movies, filmy
stings set to melt. Believe we fasted slow. When real hit its stride its pace
was to track as a body to pelt, fast marks hitting back as a belt-
splayed vein.) Outstanding image: pollen-basted body; body
in the no.

Sea change

In identical girls a group moves out
From The World to world in its other
Light. Clout. Closet we all come to
And open. Grow pinker to the spray
That mothers mine through uncolored. In
This, we are inked into. In some ways rightly
But betrayed. There is no word or entry
Or end to the engendering underwhelm
Or otherwise throated depth of them.
The girls of which I am bluntly one.
Nubby with my tucked-in two-fer moving
For to erase the redding dumbly sea. Horn
Blow your answer. Wind return to center
My legs. How do I look. How
Do I look like the hook my body even
Newly free careens towards.

Little girl walk down

That street and the side of you glinting
In light which neither
Shows nor ever will show
You your muscle, your own
Diamond face. It practices
A monument open in you, steep chamber of rock
That's becoming. Already the young sky undresses
Your body now clay, that more bendable
Fray in the either. Little, but without
Throat walk down
The tender of this slab street or glow you can't
Own, not now, in the crumbled
Seen. It is not your fault, not your
Frame twitching open, it will close
The day soon and the dread roughly
Mounts. Climb littly upon it, though
It is low get up there
Crow, girl shoes coming off
The street in clouds, invisible
Songs where you've been, legs where
You've been and strong ankles
Don't break. Code-you taps out your blessing
On the world but stomp it
Too. Flame the dress into further gold
Still sharper. There is no
Way to approach a tree, don't
Approach it. Girl string flipping
Out of you, you are turned back to blight
If you are quiet. Dust is the threat
Of being an outside
Girl and it smoothes. Your face can shine
The street you'll shine but also keep
Its water hard. Girl climb
The street as muscle thickens.
It is more than ribbon
To your lightwork.

She was my friend I sucked

She was my friend I sucked

the poison off of her heart

My stomach hurt

with powdered soups and tongue

was a burned part of me that loved her

Hid a tongue-sized prism

behind her window

Her mother

loved my diligence I grabbed her neck

Smile pulled

for fear of spiders

Dragged jam cross the homeworked weekend

Thought secrets were diamonds

through which only my shame

could rainbow out

But Animals Embody Gender Even As They Are Beyond It

Sliding down of towers, moon in tree. Men
surround me
in the early skin of my backache.
Moon in the water and landed grass
beholding. Down-sliding me
through each evening. Our boxes and down-sliding
towers, tree slickening
to cold. Oh moon, who cares
for your slick-sly down. The sky
when you slide drops down. Evening
skeins off in down-meaning
ropes. Body
with its mark. And stable,
surrounding. Grass upon which
a moon can cast light.
Circle of holding-space
light. Men
surround me
in the slide-downing sparrow. Little blow-bird with light
on its circle. A grass grows
the water darker. In flood the red knot
slips down. Silt on the moon making blood
and slid towers. Arrow of men and bird never
reaching. Down the grass which
slickens the even-so. Evening, that stiff
skin, slacks off its crust.
Heart's open bag, slag on the water.
Men
surround me,
swell of water going
green. Down-sliding
to grass and landed
towers blue. Men
surrounded me next year,
too.

A story casts for small light

I am fourteen I feel. Wanting to write

the body even enlarging.

I think of love of falling buildings.

I am back to a hand-holding hall.

Pink on the edge of the edge of my root.

A locker clicks, I kick a boy.

To see the mirror, the mirrored self.

And start the word inside.

In that sheety garden I got up high with all

the animals. Can nothing sleep in me again

if streetlights crowd the ceiling, and cars ghosting

across. I hear that dream going, that hiplift

from the river. Or, here is my river, travel me down

dark streets. Girl like a silvering, invisible ink.

I sip it closed, I sip that air right back to me.

The word starts the river, when I see her.

When she slid under the under all heat

went off. In my leg, which lay a grave.

The wall held the drips, where silence stood,

where she's going. Pray for rain

if you go. I stood at the Cube and cried

at the light. Once across going up

she put her head down.

On my shoulder, which was a music.

Go back to hell if you are.

I am standing at the square, at the light.

Come to: pink dream under blankets of press and not-sweat.

Blank of missed wet.

Her room is dried blood, dried wheat.

I wade the pile until I am close enough to _____.

Everything not smoking.

I cannot know how to be if I am a baby.

I put my angel in a basket for to fry.

Drop the deadly sea. I am rent

from old plants. Tare, as a turned bell,

bands the body. Under the orange I wait to fall

under her hands. Always story of ash.

Impossible in its onceness, and in.

Strike me, strike me, I am hunger.

Night gasps a little letter closed.

The other moon is my torn out eyelash.

In between, high violet. I move my arms

so they hurt. Have always loved the closest

rain, I stand water in till we're kissing

in closets. The frozen world is arch,

was I fourteen when I gasped.

Move your arms again.

There is that to-be-blown wish. So they hurt,

and wish for the girl.

Every tree is possession. I am past running

in the no snow. If smoke heats the box

room. What I hear is knives, no, one

tall length. It sticks when I take.

I wait this out: the nights she turns

her back back. Never climbing, never netted.

Orangish on the icing swing; precious

things. Winter ran the moon aground,

a word. That knife wonders

the wheel. I write her name so slow it will never

stop bleeding.

The frame stops the day.

Daze of catastrophe, now the smoke is travel.

Turn my turtle on and hike the slant halls.

I cannot up or spurn peak lips.

Sit on the stoop and puff till puff's cold.

Rain increases the cloud, so wet I dropped a coin in.

I tally up: all the dizzies kissed.

Wear gold when I dress this, one more death.

Sixteenth winter the fattest smudge.

Stealing rimming bottles, and smudge.

(A milk to sink my red, a blood.)

Every gray colludes with grossness.

Nothing feeling and fleet of riding.

Nothing, though I wasn't switch.

Brooklyn dropped ice, I climbed to shed the summer.

She had pink crowns and blue.

Prickle like a swallow swooping home;

or, what is lost (home):

I rub my nose on it.

And a fire to the shoulder.

Peach mallows, where I held her.

One time, and I want to be a fire.

And potent, how light entered, it almost burned, for my face was naked, held up.

In the dream she'd grown a mustache.

Stills hidden in the stand (place once walked).

To only heat part; to always explore.

A story casts (for) small light. Gray and curls.

I watch the ants go by, by.

The ink stops holding where the dead has spread its juice.

This table is tapped, a poem tacked (up).

Slips and lisps, I pulled to blush the brownstone.

Each night I kept it open.

My back, first love (first terror).

All the sheared lines (first love, and terror).

Every stretch does break, impress.

Would she touch me. She would.

Disaster

1.

I have lodged an arm.
Climb up. (And bend to block the day.)
Fringe and lint cling: I smoke it,
        smoke it. Become girl that girl
        eats, that color on the wall or color
        thrown down to starve towards.
(On the street, which lay a storm.)
Lint bubbles where static tops
        the thought of.
        (And ten kiss to stop the light.)
The memory's chopped and screwed.
I flint across time's face.

2.

The room is a garden I am not inside in.
Stable topped up with dust.
        It's an accident.
        Spin the bottle.
(Paper bag on long black hair,
        what summer heat's tied back from.)

3.

I ask for a fire.
She brings her burnt shirts.
I smell disaster on the pink water, disaster on
        the water bed.

Overture

Here she spirals to glass. Here, crook'd arm. She notches
wind to look out. Wets webs. Here is the stone standing. Wet
world. Hear a scarf unfurl in spins—the stone so like ice. Go under,
under—the isle. Flood-tunnels and egg. When whistling
bent the arrow (of the world), and when does a moth hatch. Gloss
washes the window—likewise, and wet world, and carol crisped
to tune. Then a whale song here. Here the cue is entrance, nearest
elbow, all beauteous years to scar

Entry: open road

I am a small girl. The length of me is taken by winds
to a stranger place where the air crows down. I believe
them when they tell me that. That the open word
is fallible. The large animals take the space so greenly, I lie
in the dark and more than let them. My pouts of black fur
come off in the wash then the rain comes off me and my skin
is blank with moss. The old land buckles closer in a shy
trench, the sky pasty with various almosts where the body
paged down into oil. I am a small girl, I am also prone
to the promise of weather. My ankles enter a new silver, even
the lines press me up. I feel right with it: the might. The lie lasts
itself open. There are prints the size of battered oceans, born in.
I push for greater heave, depression. But I am so small.

Wreck

Forever from the white whistling sky.

Weather moves around the buildings.

I thought I said under: the way water
moves.

Sometimes an animal leaping through the tree.

Through it, what is past, overcome.

The rain rubs that animal off.

I refuse: the dis-ease being maybe me,
what is that.

I refuse: it is not. When I am a child
protected by weather. Instead of salty

rain-steadied.

Green falls all around, blast bones
of light and wet.

I cannot bide cottony pilgrims, travelers
of sleep in my sheets.

Without drugs she points, wrapped up
in grayer stories.

Not one bang-up is easy.

I love the bruise its forgotten melt.

But when I know it I hate it.

To sit here, tapping, forbidden
from opening
the good vein . . .

Like, what if I won't.

To say right the words—the waves—
after slimming clots out.

A little spread far colorful, another night
in the apostrophe.

Being terror in its steadfastness. In its fastness.
Being nice.

Never was the stain so round.
Paper would not suffice.

There is this tremendous fear, the size
of art.

Don't pollute it.

When the ink gets down and binds it: dream
to its mean.

But I have no path,
no stretch along the robbed-out hour.

Morning is a broken end, to fill
the bell.

Water slosh. I mean, so much.

Now paint on the wooden center. Paint not being
blood, not being spinning . . .

To put it down in the rivets, the ironed-out

age. Stories maybe do this. Maybe stories
in their patness. A tree I have had is still

alive. Stories may be the reason, light
rhyme.

I pin up the downed leaves.

Stick them to the wall.

A little grassy drool on the day.

Which is no part of written:
the separation; ruination.

One puts a little spackle on.

One licks the sparkle.

One lends the song its reticence,
its reticence, partial flight.

Terror of making my mark.

Haven't I made enough marks?

I haven't made enough marks.

All the nightworms I know to be narrow.

A spider moves me past the window.

Pastness, in its arrows, full of light:
I know a sharp word when it drops.

Soot phlegm and thunder, in the waking,
which shakes sight out.

And I know a rain comes faster.
Frustrated for my lack of shaking, lack

of want.

Wrap your legs round a word
(to do that work).

But I *want* to keep the legs out.

Does the want come from fear?
(Come from hiding?)

The want not to keep slime safe.

There is not enough room.

So much room, going deep, goes
to lasting: like a fall does, dreamwards.

When I want a crippled meaning fullness
folds me down.

(Come from the posit, position.)

From the wreck, I witness

What the heart recovers

Swallow of the filter. Which falls upon you like
A burning rafter. This happened. Seminary books
Destroyed. No one thanked you
For your sweet mystery. Which swelled within them
As pollen within a pipe: soon all the taps
Sung golden with that flower. It's not that
Romantic: swallow it
Before more doves can drown in your line, or the stolen
Silk shed onto the floor in slow puddles.
At night naked the only water isn't wet, not
Really. Press that blowy photograph against your heart
Neck chest. It can light a drying fire, too, the burnish
In the less, then lost, then one last lens dressed gamely
In a red to stitch a nun to sleep. There is no picture for this:
Call the stoic what he is, expanding starch
Souring its own gluey waters. You were that water once, that yes
Steeping downwards into blue. He drew a little
Sherpa on your back. All signs pointed to the slack
Finger with which he traced your true. Black figure
Opening: this was you.

Dream sonnet

In the closed wall of dull-on night, in close
quarters to being basted, all sound's lost,
all ancients lost, all bright and glamming loss
on the floor where with all dirty clothes
piles dreaming goes faster to gone. I close
the door, close out the throng. New year: I've lost
the tune or drifted it, dreamt light in loss
down into it. What's nearer than night's close
to bone is the long unslept-on line
that, cheer girl, I've long known. There are songs
where this looks beautiful, each note lines
the floor darker to true. I wrote a song
where I almost liked it, those blues, a song
to lose hours in, to cut even bad lines.

Entry: open word

Breaks of water collapse the poisonous tongue. In the grass
Around the corner are small faces making light of the pain,
Its precedents, endingness. I have a swelling but the way I feel
Is plain, a heat slat falling. Bright pocks appear and you know
That means life squeezed too tight. There is energy to diminish
The bog, and energy to take a bland angle, pucker little fat pockets
Into clean, new fur. I hug the father though he lies in his cold
Room, limited, a pill no longer contained. By noon there is no
Rain for the feel, I have a bag of still books in this race, oh everyone
Cry for me. Photographs of beautiful women hold flat winter
Faces against the world's face. But seeing the other as always
So base deepens nothing, steel tie rusting on the table like a white
Rock being beaten. Day waves sting it, singe skin up in it. Wife
Of no sway, brand the sign of having-been-here to the side of me,
The thicker thigh crooked forward in grace, or wealth, or wait.
There is no place in the furl for a crown dying stealthily. You want
The slow collapse, the sour drip made gold by each stick of dumb
Rhyme. Slick of dumb color, there is time.

Why the heart slows

Why the area of sad futures
Is so dank. Your thighs
Stick together through every thickness.
Do not dream of faces like roads
That can be climbed. And lose points
Trying. Under the sky sickly which is always a sickly
Gray, always chiming dully.
When faces expose a loss of bone. Pocked moon
Is flatter. Then your eyes grow nothing, grow no
Image or dream. Sleep moves in
Kind, but you are not a burn. Blindly
Not. Light escapes as fat from water.
What remains of feeling and being
Felt, it is what you reach forward toward.
Your life is a pit
Expending its juice. Little bloats
Extend from it. You. That wrecked
Aloneness. There is no flora, no tonic
For the utterness of your part
Or why a root breaks out. At once this slow
And static thrash. You can continue apace,
Destroyed below the city, not seeing
How stuck each rutting thrust. Even
Here, a bad logic of lines deprives you.

Chapter

Confer to comfort: can each girl be first

Splayed by the loyal man who opened me.

Underneath whom the sea. An April full

Like hot. Hydrangeas delighting in the window.

Then winds. Then every fight of blooming jets

Through the halls and though the night was long

I can't say. Much like a puppet, yawned-past

But plastered and I was outwardly okay. A picture

With crayon wetting and tape over the owl face

Was meaning. The thing the fist of which

Could crackle anything. I fought off the beer.

I thought of a fear, and story to plant in: able, angry,

Full. I too can slick green with a kindness.

To empty the poison in. Thrashing tails and that which

Paved his sorries. I was that girl always pretty and privy.

Betrayed by my ancestry and crying O

To be under wood. Crash a day. An Apriling kid

Who'd lock down and cater. Under the world

Of him and aware of it. Did a salty powder become

The bluster. The drowned feeling. From whence

Throating. He unarched my face. And mouth nose eyes.

Each part interior, my inferior, was becoming.

Candy smoke

Nothing but blood coating the city
World, I shut and wobbled. Slow-going.
Self-steeped. A black cat
Licked the pavement. I wanted to think
It didn't miss its ear, or that water under-
Dulled the slow engine.
Light slugged closed in oranges.
Garbage garage, what sound dropped
Into: beautiful bubbling skin the sky did scar.
Once that water was the cream.
Tires rubbed their skin against the street.
I wanted the floodless
Foodless animal, to be sleep's tack,
So pressed. Halogen slurry.
The leg under the name of the loved.
Sinking was sight how I rode. Each pull
Was alone: loved—but seared light—to thicken
Luck. When a claw entered a god gull.
A knot of hair hung lowly behind it. The drug
Turned the animal into another. I try
to unarch this, the fold made secret by so telling.
Its death—god's—silvered in the median.
I wanted to be one of the men, hanging
There, listening for mine hunger so to fall.

Salt song

I wanted to feel underwater till it hurt
I wanted energy and atrophy
I wanted blue ink in my leg to redden hurt
I wanted the science to slur out
I wanted the science of slurs
Energy that it is and bubble cold
I wanted to feel ocean until hurt in cold
The violin was the sun, and clear buckets of plant
I tried not to hear them till it hurt
I wanted a cup over my head
I wanted the dream to drag honey
Stood on a rock and only heard salt
I wanted the basement a mouth opens, its plushes and tongues
And faces were layers in the sand way I wanted
Clear and cloud, the curl was the hurting
I wanted to cut a soft figure hurt
The sway, chime and blear to cast cloths cross my puddle
Cold weed of the water dragged
I wanted the little fish to swim my death
I was not a slime trail for I was not alive
I wanted to feel midnight like the sea
No one can dive

Sun

I spoke a garden through the year.
Clipped mortuary

in unseamed room.

Wedding as furnace.
The feeling numb feeling. Wrapped in a velveteen fringe.
Tassels drip
from the castle.
Body, body, say it so it's
real.

Smoke can only become
a smell. I stuck my legs
to the tracks. Kept going
in the hellbegetting bright.

Vermont '01

Small skulls in the small
skull. A sort of rounded
fever. Then the heated rises.
When the world is a grapey green
ball. A dew on the day which
sits, deposes. Don't think
a garbage higher (than it
grows). The inside tree does bend to block
the wet. It was the beat of
the parch, the beat of pink jellies.
When I cut I, the sand it
did slow.

When the heart stalls

You sit in the soup of feel and your good
Muscle starts to hurt, to lunge too thickly
Forward. Through fear you can plump
An art, deplete its endless
Mush so red sticks to blue like a righteous
Map and willing. Replenished, the day plunges
Its sticker in. If you are slick with it it is sticky
Too, dark tack lettering your fingers
In rain. You long for her and do not
Long for her, and a man comes and shows you how
To chain the spokes and in your black and broken
Dress, you do. You singe all smell
In pill. You are popped citrus and lift
Every voice. Around the circle of you your soapy
Body sets its bone. In this shift taking shape there grows
A distance, which is not the same as having meaning and a real
Book. Water drops from somewhere, so a part of you
Spins, folds back into caves. This part is the true
Part and still, you can die from it. Don't
Belong here, ever.

Center stain

What you hold into. What you hole
into. What, you hole. Wet on the mattress where
you've been. Ash on the mattress,
where you've been. Window cracked like
a cloud's ripped skull. And wet on the wall. And scratch
on the walls where you've been. Having been
foggy and matted. Having a mattress
on the round floor. And wet on the floor.
Your body round
on the floor. And wet on the floor where
you've babied, a baying.
A bread given purpose, where you've
been, thread past night. A thing
of old light. Your thin risen out from. Been cloudy
and flesh. And a floor is your skin
what it's been, depressed in. Out the window
been brick. And white
as brick folds. In the mirror cracked open
some white, being ground. Thus been puffy
in mess. All being and flush in the skin having
flesh. Been past being full to being
flat sadly. Mattress opened
of sheet. And day opened
of sheet. And what are the boxes, you
are that they heel. Been knees' inside creak.
Having pressed into heat. Gone flat
in red marks being pushed, pressed
to rip. Corners in stain, having listened,
sat splat in, redressed, what it looks. What walks
down the street to being in starker.
What walks, even. Not slimming, not slime.
And knowing the room, being born
from the room.

Season

I took to scrubbing mirrors, a sheared smile-wrenching
feeling. Each gnat a gun flap. Afternoons I'd hit
the volume so volume'd outscreen me. I edged the Eiffel,
could isolate hips. And when you breathe, She said, Feel
your belly, hated bowl. What I took to loving
was a soupy laugh and willingness to swell.
Every mistake I've made, every knot uphilled
in ether. Shaved one thing; grew the other.
Wasn't my mother but cat-cowed crumbs
from the floor. I took that fall so greenly even eggs
agreed with me. No math to volley. No rock
at the door.

Vodka song

Love could not make me sick.
My eyes could not make me sick.
Sitting on the pants-tattering rocks.
A sound slipped to smellessness.
Afternoon endless. Ethering to kissing
in the unsubtle street. Behind the curtain
I pulled off my bra as her, name
as her. Pulled the velvet like rubbing
someone else's dream. Maybe writing
the girl is always touching a piano
sticky fingers have touched. I feel the juice
where a body ghosted off into fruit, slack
over this bite with this tongue.

Where the voices were

There is a whole amount, that is not what I want.
Twiddling thumbs and the way they slid down sorry.
A little nod-off: *I am bored, I am bored, I am nice*, grown
From the back of the bus to couch. I doubled over
When that back grew lousy and eggless. No part of me
Knew it, how to cushion, defrag the claws out. In motherless
Time I growled, breasty-empty (goblined). It was a good time.
They were good years. Head apportioned to the wall, where
The voices were.

Last song

Searched the pilgrim climb
to cave again. Doved open in a beastly weather. Unbothered by trial, by carving,
celebration. I sat upon the smoked-up blue, on tilt with sleep. Word so much
a cut it threaded rain.
Faster of fever.
Knocked before was found.
I was never so sharp I bore silence. Mirage
of illness, what sung the sloe hang.
Throat gulfed fear aground.
I tongued my tooth—hole home—down,
sat upon a climb, a woman kept from stone
and still light shuddered in the knife-lit dawn.

What the heart hides

You are as blank as a long white brick. A tablet.
A pill of earth that your tongue presses down.
You equate nothing with nothing, with a gradual
Sort of greatness, a gradation of weather on the backlit
Broken porch. In your hands is some coolness—do nothing
With it. Do the dirt that your century upholds
As real, as raw, as replete with blued blood. If you cannot
Be good, be leather, that rich and flat. Aware of no
Throathold. Cabled in clinched
Kisses. Across the street a man
Swings his arms around. Be that man, as bold, gored
Out. Once you were a clear stout cup. You rattled
With drink and puddled
As fast. Nights muddied you and you
Moved out from them, trued to no softer
A river, boy, or woman. Sometimes your neck
Crept with shadow, and you could not
Breathe, and liked it. You could not breathe
And liked it, and liked the smoke sweetening
Inside of you. If you have known rooms
They have known you, your wetness and flattened
Affect, your mood hanging
The air thick, thicker, still
Thicker than that.

I want that which is closed

and that witch with her clothes unwrapped. I want the sugar
of it all abouting around me: the table and the cinnamon
stick, that boy bleating outwardly, to and through, without.
I want the lone hair who itches. The which-ones-are-those,
though they depress me like the dickens. Mixing eggs very
cleanly. The dirty less the dirt. I want to be so old I vomit
with it, my skin a crusty paper napkin. It disgusts me, all of:
the litany, the line with no minus, every dry thing crimping
prematurely at its ankles. The sun is a sad sort of white.
It makes me can't breathe. I want the smell again, the faint
again, the red scorching of knees. Summer pots its scratchy
beads but the bright bride is tired. Besides the lack of burn
she is tired. If there was a seed for my feeling it would be
closed. I would want it. I would want the bitter belch of its
world, and there is (it's crystal), and I do.

Rewilding

What is on fire.
 A rock.
What is on fire.
 Lines that are turning.
What is on fire.
 The death that flies draw.
What is on fire.
 Woven no fray.
What is on fire.
 The end of all knots.
What is on fire.
 Architecture.
What is on fire.
 Fear.
What is on fire.
 An animal eats the hole.
What is on fire.
 Killing the wolves.
What is on fire.
 Sparks.
What is on fire.
 Stolen white sage.
What is on fire.
 He burned off her eyes.
What is on fire.
 The name and the know.
What is on fire.
 Further in ink.
What is on fire.
 Singing the legs.
What is on fire.
 The dust of old days.
What is on fire.
 A shallow sound.

What is on fire.
>   Learning so quiet.
What is on fire.
>   Timekeeping.
What is on fire.
>   Elbows hit with time.
What is on fire.
>   Shame's swaddle.
What is on fire.
>   Falling paper.
What is on fire.
>   The smell in the village.
What is on fire.
>   Pinkish shavings.
What is on fire.
>   Knowing one's mother.
What is on fire.
>   Crass mall ligature.
What is on fire.
>   The article.
What is on fire.
>   Throated with wine.
What is on fire.
>   Freshing the dumb out.
What is on fire.
>   Not feeling the body.
What is on fire.
>   Love and light as necessary ends.

Home

There is no place left.
The sparrow slides into the new store.
A wall beside the street, it is where the newness
That is my body rests.
I put my nose in it.
Love, the orange fever.
Apartment of waltzes, I am naked with
The once girl. My mother feeds the starlings,
But death grows. Vicodin and fire
Escape. Uptown the village
Turns to plastic. Candy clouds dress strollers
In death. All the people pushed. Light just
Razed it.

It was the middle of the end,
A story about to move.
Teeth past holes, disaster pickled.
I cannot afford it: loving home,
A block and a bic.
My throat hurt her belly, that I sang.
There is no place left, the memory
A calamity box.

And it is night, the shell breaks . . .

Lion song

A girl in the bottle in drawers. Stories deep as stories
fold. I took the path as steam departed, a little lightning
shoulder. Steam departed without gift. Unscrewed
safety drifted, lifted, lifting through such cold. No song
to plod or ancient stringing. Paths from drawers I thought
I hung. I thought insurance tucked in stories. The lips
of which caught steam on lightning. There was the dance
in basements. Windows of light and water. A girl a bottle
lipped, the wake up when the clouds are low. Soot drawn
to wake an orange. I tongued that path till light down
shifted. Blue animal in the wrecked blue. Cold took the path,
and time moved. The folded open path prolonged
the steam through which I mucked some story. A lion
and an empty. Headed from security. I would not buzz to
remember. But someone is singing, thank god

Night, a root

The bells grow before me. I stick my egg in a flower.
Everywhere I have tried to look: for covenant. For to extinguish
the thought. Sleet kept me looking when I traveled
in a walk. I took a pill when the bus took darkness.
Where am I? The fish rots in the bag. Tomorrow we will eat
the fish. The room of windows is happy and still.
Bells are a family too, full of holiday feeling.
I cannot slide deeper than having kidsistered the sleigh,
for to extinguish the bell takes vibrato from wrists. What I never
learned: an energy to sit saying nothing. Not slit, no punch—
nothing. I have been angry as a geyser has, which is to say my feeling
is so integral as to be stateless, to say it pretty a cruelness
past pin. I have tried. Now I worry the day grows lighter.
The night before the bus is longer, its edges heaving
to morning to slap. It feels a sludge, the cigarette
on the step beside the station. When I have tried, alone,
to steed the temper—cold rip. Blue as the wood's edge,
moon under cloud coming in, in, in.

Overture

Hatch bulb. And thicket. A little swell on the roofed-off
rising. Being been dark. Round down and rush. A slight a stable
grazes, then raises. The night the raining curtained the wind the wind
rose back. All ears to the ground—all fur. What can be dismantled
as a spider starts to scratch

Page which depletes and denies

Take the forest which is wet
The letter between the legs   A tower is a night rising up.
Streets will with breaks.   Be normal logic: the mouth.
The mouth twisting its logic.   Between the flare and the forest,
                                     Letters fill. And wet.

    I do believe the street
    Legs twist. Logic flares this.
    Teach it to the mouth,   What travels. In the arch
    That arrow. Forests and letters.   And the specter. The dark bloom
                                            Teaches its letters. Logic which
                                            Leaves, drop down
        I want to write normal.
        Believe the bloom rising up,
        I do. With the energy of a flare.
        It teaches the night a tower.   A tower a night rising up.
                                            Wetly teach it in the so-called
      Light. There are legs in this Light. The normal one,
      And the specter. The legs   And the street, and the arch
      In the street are letters. Speak
      Kindly to them. A soft bloom

           In the mouth. It is still
        In dark letters flares The room to me. I do believe
        In dark letters. The fill in normal forests, and in taking
        Blooms wet. Between what's wet.
        Legs and a street which is

          Wet is a tower.   Is I want to write
          The mouth the end. Is my I leaving a dropping
          Down. The street's normal logic, but
          The energy. The kindly. Taken in, the twisting

Nothing in my mouth.
A bloom of logic in a forest of letters darkens,
Means nothing. Leaves, drop down my mouth
If a street is a mouth till an arrow breaks open
                    In the after-specter.

I write normal wants.
The legs and the tower,
The cripple of light rising   Is I want to write higher
Up. It is still. It is still.   A travel. Or is it normal
                    Through its flares and taken.
The mouth flares   Filling nothing.

The mouthflares   Fill nothing.

What the heart seals

You slant your flangey cup down. Grow fatter
In the bland unbeastly thicket. There is no fire
To true center: your cut flattened
With ash, each embalming steadfast
In its muck. In a fruit's self-stiffening
Circle a gold may crust open
In furious spores or glassed in
Light grow long. A girl in the grass lies
Closer, blond and blond
As a dream. In her wiving mind she shrouds whole
Planets. If she slides lace it is lace
That you need, for you are tired,
Every cloud enlarges, no, enrages
You. Are you sad your sadness is a sheet she air
Dries, smoothes down so it can be touched
Again by corners, touch in its gummy
Loathing so flattened. Has this been said to you? You
Have said this. In the field a horse
Is not mold or rust but brass and if you beam
Too he may know you too. That girl you are also
Is here and rub off
Her ditchy skin. What fills with fresh
Water will heal its own splinters then flanked
By good fur be found. Now you are not
A thing. This is not to say
You are nothing. Even and only in this shadow and lift
Can you open. The girl leans nearer—*can you every*
In her field really fit?—in the grass,
Sweat or silk, your body generous real,
Unfettered finally by how much
You have hated it.

The Last Night

in the apartment I stayed up.
Everything gone. Everything
except everything
I'd written: loving a girl, a shoulder
in singe. Village doused in wet dawn.

I was sixteen that fall.
By spring, almost done.

That night I didn't paint over
the wall. I didn't
have a knife.
I wrote the sweet year
into my arm. Alive.

Middle song

There is no beautiful midnight.
There is no beautiful morning.

The dark has been beautiful.
There is no beautiful morning.

Morning was beautiful when she came.
The night was long and dark.
There is no beautiful morning.

There is no thing to sharp dark.
An hour, a middle, a song.
There is no beautiful morning.

The night was dull and long.
Morning, ended.
Lines love a beautiful edge.
There is no beautiful midnight.

Lateness trades on blue, its song.
The middle there is easy.
The song unfolds to spider.
There is no easy ending.

Ease is not so beautiful,
so seamed a sweet-round middle.
The lines wanted that late edge.
There is no hour not late.

The night gripped through with beauty.
Lines heaved in the morning line.
There is no beautiful midnight.
There is no beautiful morning.

I remember standing

on a cliff